FOLLOWING THE FIRSTBORN

A PILGRIM'S PROGRESS IN PICS AND POEMS: 1970-2020

JIM WARD

Ark House Press
PO Box 1722, Port Orchard, WA 98366 USA
PO Box 1321, Mona Vale NSW 1660 Australia
PO Box 318 334, West Harbour, Auckland 0661 New Zealand
arkhousepress.com

Unless otherwise stated, all Scriptures are taken from the New Living Translation
(Holy Bible. New Living Translation copyright© 1996, 2004, 2007, 2013 by
Tyndale House Foundation. Used by permission of Tyndale House Publishers
Inc., Carol Stream, Illinois 60188. All rights reserved.)

Some names and identifying details have been changed to protect the privacy of
individuals.

Cataloguing in Publication Data:
Title: Following the Firstborn
ISBN: 978-0-6489912-2-9 (pbk)
Subjects: Memoir; Photography;

Design by initiateagency.com

CONTENTS

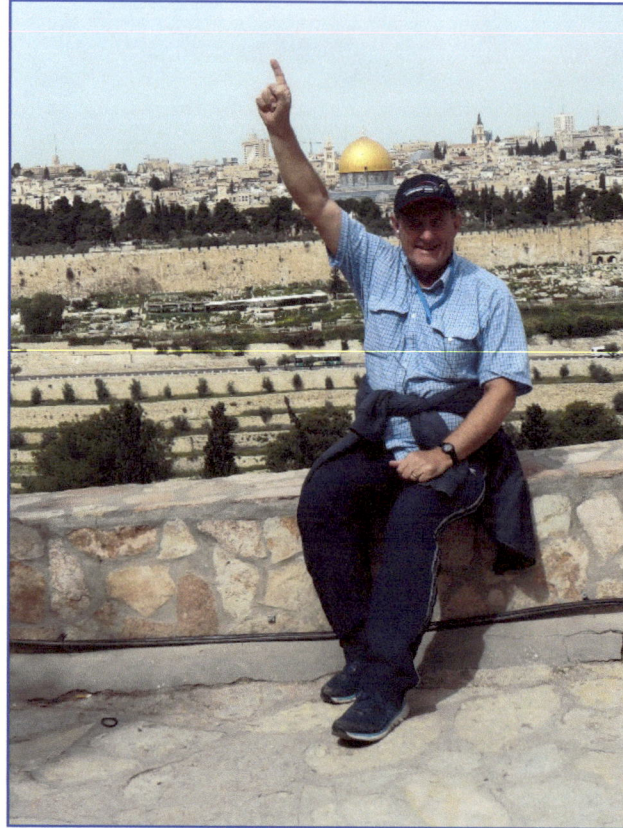

He is the head of the body, the church;
He is the beginning and the firstborn from among the dead,
so that in everything He might have the supremacy.

Colossians 1:18

INTRODUCTION

This book is the result of four passions – travel, photography, poetry and being a follower of Jesus.

It has been a privilege over the last half century to explore this world, photograph some of its wonders and signposts to truth and then write reflectively about it. This has led to learning more about its Creator, who is revealed specifically in His Word. His blessings naturally compel one to want to share with others something of the lasting fulfilment discovered in following Jesus the 'Firstborn' from the dead.

There are ten of my poems here that have been inspired by sights and events that have burst upon the senses, often at quite unexpected moments, over the last fifty years as I have tried to follow the Firstborn. Each poem invites consideration of an important aspect of the progress of a contemporary Christian pilgrim. These aspects are reflected, developed and illuminated in facing page photographs I have taken – all except one - but more of that later.

The discerning reader who explores how the photographs develop and focus the themes established by the poetry, can expect rich rewards of new insights to truth.

The ten thematic strands sequence a growing understanding of the plan of salvation for all human beings that was heralded in the first Noel. Each is a crucially important topic to a Christian pilgrim progressing forwards in maturity, and as such invites reflection personally, and in discussion with others.

A growth discussion group could use each one of these ten topics to explore the progress of a pilgrim through life. Each topic culminates in a significant faith question. Thoughtful investigation of the answers found in the secrets of the Firstborn can lead one through the labyrinth of false trails towards fruitful truth.

The Reflection Guide provides starting points for pilgrim navigation and also some 'backpack' resources to help cope with the inevitable exigencies on the track ahead.

If we are brave enough to 'ask and seek' honestly with regard to these questions there can only be a deepening of our understanding, not only of this world but also of its Creator, who is infinitely concerned for our well-being within it and beyond.

Jim Ward 2020.

Sloop through the Storm

Oh, listen to the song of the fussing foam,
As rudder bubbles dance to the high wind moan;
The cleated sheet hums in harmony and onwards we roam.

You invade the lavender lace maelstrom, with salt sleepy eyes that see the spray's
Intimation of power, and the tiller becomes a tiger –
One moment it is silently supple and then a thrashing craze,
Fighting to master the exhilarated rider.

Many, cunning as a spider with web crushed,
Spin yet again for the self, with all sense oblivious
To this Creator's song of awesome strength or the lessons of a former hour
That might warn of ignominious shipwreck, certain and supercilious.

So it is that passion is unleashed, Oh beware, sailor unwary;
It gusts unexpectedly to test us either as a fluttering feather
Or well-tuned hull driven hard – two spirits contrary.
They do battle as the heart learns to triumph over hard weather.

At length, eyes become slits that glimpse endless liquid hills to climb,
And, tossed helplessly now, hope almost fails, yet suddenly, Oh serenity sublime,
The homeport light flashes across a sturdy bow, now steadfast in time.

On completing secondary school in 1970.

Tiberius on the west coast of the Sea of Galilee. Nazareth is higher behind. Jesus ministered here.

Reconstruction of a Galilean fishing boat.

Mosaic of a famous storm, which Jesus quelled.

Remains of a Galilean boat dating to the time of Jesus.

QUESTION 1:   Do I have the faith to trust Jesus through the storms of life?

Girl whose times are a changing...

There once was a girl with long dark hair,
Melancholy was her name.
Few glimpsed the beauty
of her face so fair
In moments when free from pain.

Worry and sadness reduced
her to the "madness"
And old Satan did chuckle in glee,
From thought to thought he
did wickedly oppress
That girl who means so much to me.

Valiant was her stand but alas, alone,
Anguish usurped her face;
Murmuring defeat in a melancholic tone
She seemed to give up her race.

But all praise and glory be
to God our Father,
Who helps us in our distress,
For He can lift us up from the miry pit
Whenever we are lost in a mess.

I have beheld a wondrous change,
As God dispelled the gloom,
Eyes of faith now lovingly range
And a merry light fills her room.

Revealed is a jewel so precious,
Who rests with God always,
With infinite strength, her
fight is victorious,
For she is one with Him whom we praise.

Many there are who have this sadness
Of trying to fight alone;
Grief will their joyful spirit suppress,
Until they make Christ, their home.

Written for an orphaned girlfriend, suffering sadness and depression: 30 September 1972.

Veiled lady, sculpture -
Chatswood House, UK.

Grecian lady, sculpture -
British Museum, UK.

A brave girl openly surveys infinity from the perspective of Wedding Cake Rock, south of Sydney.

QUESTION 2:   What veils our views and needs surgery by the Master?

Luke by the Lake

It was early morning when
the tussle began,
Down by the lake between
Geneva and Lausanne.
We were heading out, His Spirit and I,
For the shore of that water
where the big steamers ply.

My backpack was squeaking
at the stumbling pace,
Of sleepy legs, striding out
a latecomer's race.
After a hot, restless night I
had missed the rising sun,
And hurrying like this was
ruining my fun.

I wish I had woken up early -
In time for a wash, shave and
other things loved dearly –
Like reading Luke – Ah – but
… well, you see, instead …
I spent just far too long in bed.

There was only about a mile to go
under a summer sun, already boiling,
When His voice came into my
head, rhythmically calling:
'My son, the race cannot be won
Unless your reading work is done.'

'Oh no, please not now,' I moaned,
And it seemed like every muscle groaned;
'Later, when I'm sitting
on board that boat,
I'll get the book out and
read what Luke wrote.'

Back came the reply in His
soft, steady tone:
'Use this quiet walk whilst we're alone,
And so be strong to walk your talk,
'Tis too late when all the
trials make you balk.'

Surely my busy day had begun, although
deep down I knew He was right.
I, however, was not giving
in without a fight:

'But… I'm hot, tired and late,
And besides, Luke is in the pocket of my
pack on my sweaty back, MATE!'

Why was there a lonely, empty feeling inside?
Suddenly, I wanted to run away and hide.
These angry words for my greatest friend –
Was I really His, now and to the end?

And so it was, with many a contortion,
That, I reached right around my bulky proportion,
And through some timely, phenomenal fluke,
I extracted that elusive gospel of Luke.

And the people passing by noticed with amazement,
A strange figure moving down the pavement;
Reading and walking, self-will in pieces,
He was rapt in the wondrous words of Jesus.

Written overlooking alpine splendour near Kandersteg, Switzerland, whilst backpacking: 25 June 1976

West shore of the Lake of Galilee looking north towards where Jesus taught on the Mount.

Jordan River where many are baptised daily into following the Firstborn.

QUESTION 3: What do I make of Jesus today - who is He and how does He become my personal friend?

Palmetum Musing – a school excursion.

A busload of poets, that's a laugh!
These rollicking students are a
rabble as we seek a new path,
And instead of quietly
anticipating nature's pearls,
Mischievous hormones merely
show off to giggling girls.

But then, after we'd wandered
and sat down a bit,
A calmer, balmy acceptance saw
each scratch for some wit;
Palm soothed by a changed
pace of swaying fronds,
Magic words found their place
from the eternal bard beyond.

The back-lit sheens of sunlit greens,
Shed refreshing shade over
awakening faces
Locking in now to sharp rain smell
under puffy new cloud wafts.
A few notice when the first
thirsty blade of grass leans
Towards the distant lace
Of a luxurious, showery trace.

Assaulted by a savage dry season,
this Palmetum is a test,
Set by those who water and tend
it, whilst all around the rest
Dies, drought stricken in brown despair;
Just like us, if we waste our
opportunities, being there.

An English Writing Excursion – mid 1990s: Encouraging creative writing amongst the young is always a challenge to sharpen the senses and insights to the Creator's hand, especially amidst the clamour of city life. This school excursion during drought conditions to a charming oasis of palms in a tropical city, saw two English teachers strive to link empathy with intricate expression. The respectful, animated tones on the returning bus were in stark contrast to the initial churlishness. Like cicadas who have shed their ugly exoskeletons, new stars were born to pierce the unrelenting heat with song.

South Coast,
Royal National
Park, NSW.

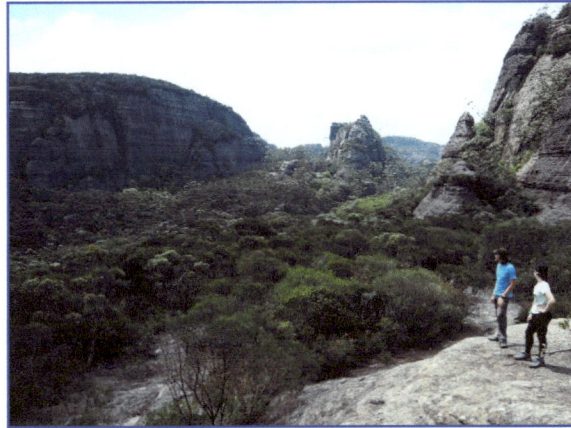
Monolith Valley,
Budawang Mountains,
southern NSW.

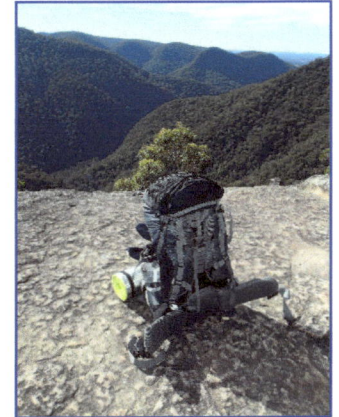

Central NSW falls,
tucked away
in forest.

Graceful gums
encountered in the
Blue Mountains,
NSW.

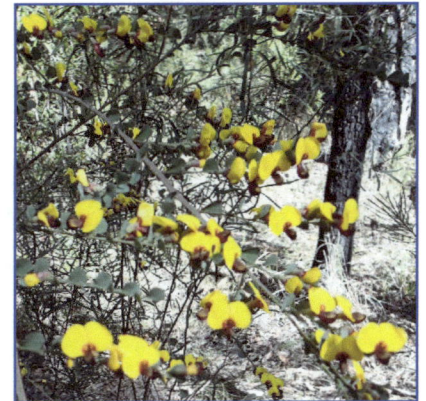

QUESTION 4: How perceptive is my view of the Creator's handiwork?

Heavy Homecoming

Oh Father, my death is too heavy;
Without you, how can I bear all this?
Our planet has become vicious, especially when they hiss
At my shame. Oh my people, I despise the cruelty you levy.

Torturers, you think this but sport,
To raise the vinegar of your impudent gall and prolong
My horrendous spasms of final earth song.
Oh how lonely, Father, is their scorn that my trust in you has bought?

Know, rebels, that it is you who are caught in the snare,
You have missed the secret of My Kingdom:
The wonderful news of my Father's peace, good will and welcome.
So many of you will be lost forever, Oh tragic thought.

But … there is going to be such joy in the new dawn …

I am first to be reborn! Yes, free! Followed by millions of forgiven others,
For those who trust in me will become my sisters and brothers.
Soon…yes so soon…we'll celebrate … and without end…
Father … we're coming … for I … am both … their Lord … and … friend.

A poem written on a contemplative College Easter Staff retreat in the 1990s, where a brave chaplain defied constraints of both inscrutable liturgy and secular expectations of complacency and simply encouraged all present to empathise creatively with Jesus on the cross.

Gnarled survivors. Olive trees can live for thousands of years. These ones photographed in the garden of Gethsemane in 2019 may well have eavesdropped on some of the most important words ever spoken:

"My Father, if it is possible, may this cup be taken from me. Yet not as I will, but as you will."Matthew 26:39.

QUESTION 5:   What inheritance does Jesus offer to us as a free gift and how do we claim it?

Expectation of Revival

Crackling around ancient walls and silent, solid rafters at this hour
There is promise of your work, precious Spirit;
There comes a sudden, surging fire of transporting power -
An exhilarating moment of truth is here and all will feel it.

Complacent ears are now compelled to shake
Before the stupendous call of gospel love 'quake,
Willing elders who have prayed long for fertile soil, weeded of all worldly excuse,
Will exult, that after long nights of vigil, new birth is let loose.

Oh yes! Here the Spirit comes, with flawless, diamond love to light the pastor's face,
Suffusing the earnest smile with joy and kindling mighty works of grace.
Oh Spirit, hide the sad, proffered histories of those called to kneel here,
And fill them with angel-song of the love that casts out all fear.

There is always a waning as the afterbirth pulse of healing balm
Fades, along with the touches of counselling hand on arm;
But now everywhere, gospel love chorus swells all the more, despite life's disarray,
And leads many chosen others to the heavenly way.

October 2002
An epiphany of renewal, inspired by an old, church building, with magnificent roof rafters of splendidly worked wood, which would no doubt have been appreciated by a certain carpenter father from Nazareth – and his son.

Many come from all over the world to be baptised in the Jordan River. Here, there is an ethereal, transcendent harmony of brothers and sisters, who, each in their own language, promise allegiance to the Firstborn. It is an exhilarating multi-lingual vibe that filters enticingly across the pristine waters and flowered banks of that symbolic watercourse, where once upon a time, Jesus Himself was baptised.

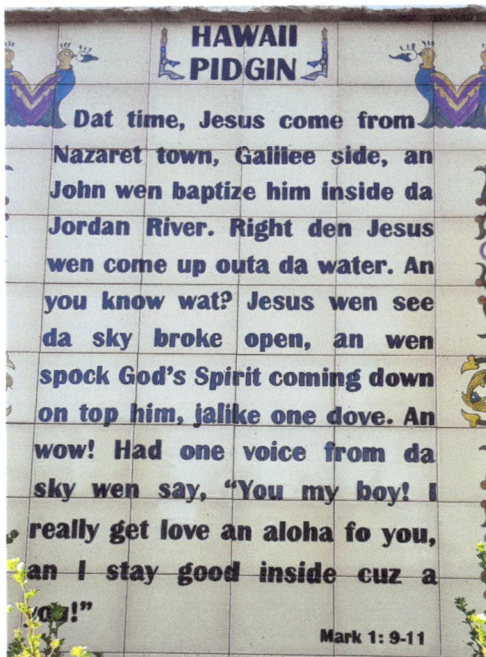

Baptism of the Firstborn – in Pidgin

HAWAII PIDGIN

Dat time, Jesus come from Nazaret town, Galilee side, an John wen baptize him inside da Jordan River. Right den Jesus wen come up outa da water. An you know wat? Jesus wen see da sky broke open, an wen spock God's Spirit coming down on top him, jalike one dove. An wow! Had one voice from da sky wen say, "You my boy! I really get love an aloha fo you, an I stay good inside cuz a you!"

Mark 1: 9-11

QUESTION 6: Have we discovered that the Kingdom of Christ can eliminate conflict and selfish greed, so that we can in fact all be one in Him, across every political, racial and cultural divide?

Blossoming

Your smile amongst rich autumnal hues at Blackheath,
Remained with me, calm as a cyclone's eye, through this sad winter,
And although that unhappy season stole the glorious leaf,
You promise a spring that will replace what was bitter.

Your fierce love, so precious and dear,
Is etched true in the deserts of lonely anguish,
So now with the help of Him with whom perfect love casts out fear,
Let us embrace a new way forward, fulfilling only His wish.

This earthly journey means both pain and pleasure,
But beside me, love, let us serve to find God's favour,
For He pours out treasure beyond measure;
Thus united, the blossoms will flourish, and we will not waver.

On rejuvenating retreat at leafy Blackheath in the Blue Mountains, NSW, after rejection and bitterness in the workplace: October 2002.

Spring blossoms in the Blue Mountains cause one to gasp in the presence of such intricate loveliness. These are signposts to the very character, essence and magnificence of the Godhead.

QUESTION 7: How can we remember blossoms of hope and renewal when winters of setback and loss seduce us to despair?

Remembering Tanya – Heaven's Happy Foal...

And in heaven they shall gambol with joy like a new born foal… (Anon)

You floated far above the
how and the why,
Imbued with the same passionate
acumen that your Saviour knew -
Fiery justice decisively
toppling each derelict lie,
But the gentlest empathy and
care, embracing me and you.

The soft, compelling lilt of
your powerful words,
Surrounds us still to inspire, assuage
and penetrate the core of every issue;
Each cyclonic tumult then yields its
soft eye and we are set free as birds,
Finding healing, proportion and a
bridge to cross every troubling fissure.

To you was given the gift
of prophetic vision,
Crisp, clear insight to motive and means,
So honestly shared regardless
of all worldly collision,
That in knowing you we
grow straight and strong.

How hard you have worked for others
dear sister, teacher, wife and mother,
Not sparing yourself amidst the
wrenching anxieties of many roles;
So with this sweet memory of deep
sacrifice we may encourage one another,
Now that a beloved daughter is released
home – one of heaven's happy foals.

With a gravely ill husband and beset by desperately heavy demands as both a Senior English Teacher and a Pastoral Care Coordinator of a Year 12 cohort about to graduate, colleague Tanya's generous heart gave out and she died on World Teacher Day, November 2016. She had dedicated herself perceptively and unstintingly to meeting the needs of her students, as she prayed and longed for each one to know the Lord.

Tanya's workstation after she went home. So strange to pass by and remember her.

Superbly groomed horses graze happily in fertile peace and luxury under an English summer sun. They were photographed with a zoom lens from the walls of Middleham Castle, Yorkshire, where the son of a certain great King Richard was born.

The sad death of this son, just before that of his mother and then his father on the battlefield of civil war, was yet one more human trail of tragedy but it had dire consequences for the realm.

For followers of the Firstborn, however, all flaws of our humanity can be healed and then forgotten. Unhappy repercussion is then replaced by the sheer bliss and secure vitality of eternal life with Jesus. Ultimately, there is a way to perfection for each of us, and scarlet sins can be washed clean as snow.

Oh Happy Day – Jesus has banished the sting of death away. Parting is only 'au revoir' for those following the Firstborn. A victory feast awaits.

QUESTION 8:   How brightly does the hope of eternal life burn for me?

A Scientist Stays the Course

No, you were never over the hill
But kept pressing onward, onward still.
Though this world is much changed from where your youth has been,
Your hunt for the big brave answers was forever honest and keen.

The personal computer, smart phone and GPS
Were unknown to the science that first knew your best;
But they were revealed along with the other secrets of your lore,
Where discovery was no child of pride but forged with awe.

Each year now clangs to a doubtful close,
With little sense of Empire, new frontiers and the welfare of human beings,
Upon whom your science sought to bestow safety, security and amazing dreams -
Lost today in greedy mass media babble, increasingly absurd.

Undaunted to the end you stood strong for the faith, hope and love of divine truth,
Following the gleam of certainty emanating deep within
That one day soon you would meet the very Creator of all this, yes Him!
Big questions are now answered by the perfect Designer, no longer aloof.

And so this narrow path makes all the difference as onward we also must press,
Choosing either lethargy or faithful pilgrim in service no less.

In 1994 I wrote a poem of admiration and encouragement to my Physicist father for his consistent reconciliation of science with his faith, amidst an agnostic and materialistic, self-seeking age. The elements of that poem became the core of this one, written over some years after he passed home in 2013, aged 94.

Two great symbols of scientific achievement – France's Eiffel Tower, Paris, and England's *Great Britain* steel ship - preserved now in Bristol. It had many innovations to make travel safer and was modified late in its design to utilize the revolutionary invention of the propeller. There is great national pride here.

$$E = mc^2$$

This photograph was not taken by the author but by his radio physicist father in 1972. It records his invention of a new over the horizon radar design, standing sentinel over the tropical city of Townsville, North Queensland, on what is now the splendid Kissing Point Museum Reserve. It could track dangerous cyclones thousands of kilometres away but was eventually superseded by satellite technology. Scientists following the Firstborn quietly get on with studying the Creator's world and harnessing its secrets for the good of others. They give the glory to God, knowing that although science can help us, it will not ultimately save us. There is great humility here.

QUESTION 9:   Of what truth should we be proud - will it stand the test of time?

Small Steps and a Giant Leaps – mother zooms home.

Consider a mother who is like the Command Module
Of an Apollo Space Mission –
She is blasted towards discovery and shelter
In many alien environments
By huge forces and stages according to an intricate plan.

Much dross mother shed in propulsion towards incredible
Moments of mercy, service and witness for her controller, Jesus.

Scarred and pitted, she zoomed for Him in triumph.

Now at rest in her joyful peace, there is transcendence for all to see:

Her mission was accomplished.

October 2019 – completed after the interment of mother's ashes.
Aged 94 in Queensland, whilst the author was travelling in the UK in May of 2019, mother passed peacefully away after serving her Lord faithfully without faltering, since she was a young girl. She trained to be a doctor in London during the blitz, served on the mission field in the wild interior of Borneo and carried her clear, practical Christian light to succour many through the confused educational and medical fogs of an Australia at the end of the twentieth century, that was groping to find a way forward through gathering schism and existentialism.

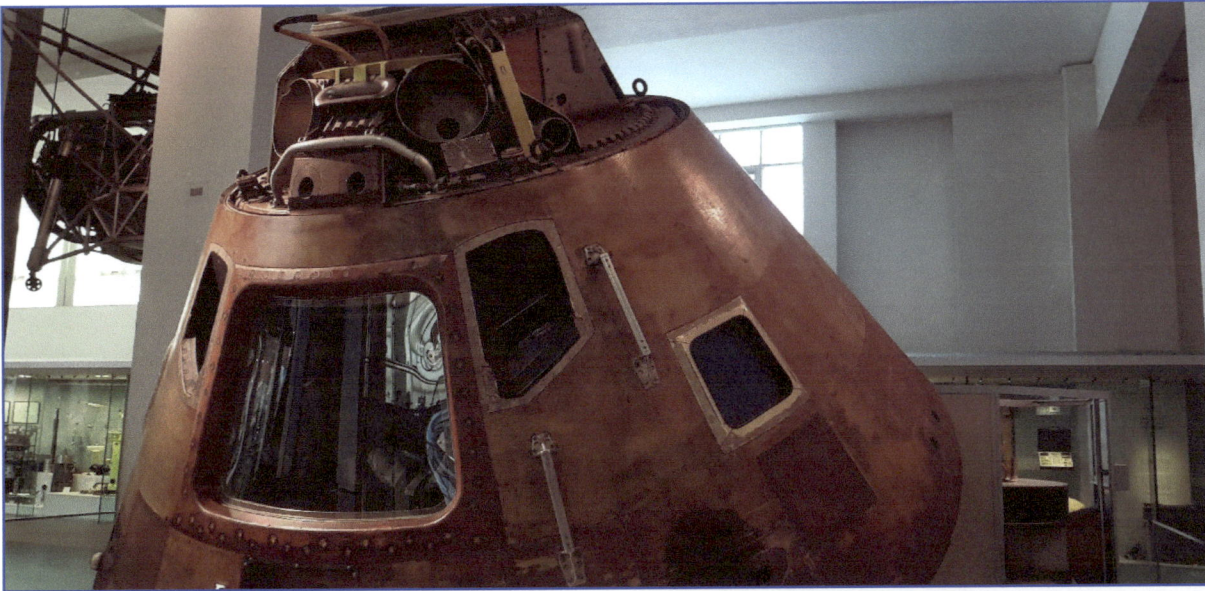

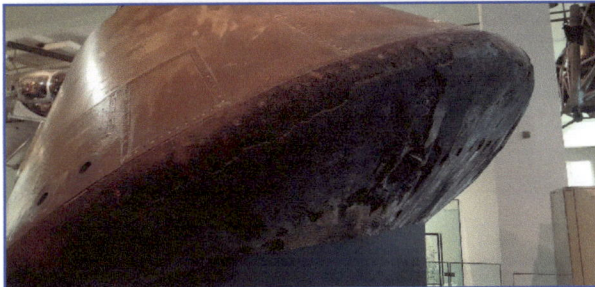

Charlie Brown is the Apollo 10 Command Module re-entry capsule, which is now displayed in an innocuous corner of the Science Museum, London. As he was being photographed, it seemed to the author that he was murmuring victoriously that he had been to the moon and back … so there … think on that! It was humbling to think of what had been achieved and the silent triumph of this mission over awesome challenges involving unbelievable forces. The next mission highlighted the successful first moonwalk.

Also grieving, but in joyful thanks over a mother who had just gone peacefully home on the other side of the planet, I looked more closely at Charlie and suddenly, a poem was born. There is a great tranquillity of the soul in knowing the joy of walking under the perfect control of the Firstborn, who, for those who trust and obey Him, cares, guides and supports with perfect timing in every venture no matter how overwhelming it might seem at first.

QUESTION 10:   Do the deep peace and joy of Jesus sustain and propel me on His missions 'impossible'?

EPILOGUE

This famous pilgrim poem is the only one positively attributed to John Bunyan who wrote *The Pilgrim's Progress*. It first appeared in 1684 in part two of his famous progress book.

The Pilgrim is inspired by the reference in Hebrews 11:13 to the fact that God's chosen people "confessed that they were strangers and pilgrims on the earth."

It is here because all who truly follow the Firstborn are pilgrims in transit who know of this hope and resolve.

The Pilgrim

Who would true valour see
Let him come hither;
One here will constant be,
Come wind, come weather.
There's no discouragement,
Shall make him once relent,
His first avowed intent,
To be a Pilgrim.

Who so beset him round,
With dismal stories,
Do but themselves confound;
His strength the more is.

No lion can him fright,
He'l with a giant fight,
But he will have a right,
To be a Pilgrim.

Hobgoblin, nor foul fiend,
Can daunt his spirit:
He knows, he at the end,
Shall Life inherit.
Then fancies fly away,
He'l fear not what men say,
He'l labour night and day,
To be a Pilgrim.

John Bunyan

REFLECTION GUIDE

Each poem focuses us on a response to an important life challenge. It provides a context for searching. The pictures and reflections then lead us to key questions that can guide us towards crucial truths. Are we brave enough to 'knock so the door will open, to seek so that we might find'? Matthew 7:7.

Contents – ten big questions for the progress of today's pilgrim:

1. ***Sloop through the Storm*: Facing the storms.**
   Do I have the faith to trust Jesus through the storms of life?

2. ***Girl Whose Times are a' Changing*: Revealing truth behind veils.**
   What veils our views and needs surgery by the master Creator and Sustainer?

3. ***Luke by the Lake*: The unique fulfilment of a personal relationship with Jesus.**
   What do I make of Jesus today? Who is He and how does He become my personal friend? Does the thought of Him ruin or make my fun? What interaction do I have with Him?

4. ***Palmetum Musing – a school excursion*: Learning to read the imprint of our Creator.**
   How perceptive is my view of the Creator's handiwork in the universe around us?

5. ***Heavy Homecoming*: Inheriting a priceless future.**
   What inheritance does Jesus offer to us as a free gift and how do we claim it?

6. ***Expectation of Revival*: All One in Christ – for all the followers of the Firstborn.**
   Have we discovered that the Kingdom of Christ can eliminate conflict and selfish greed, so that we can in fact all be one in Him: one family across every political, racial and cultural divide?

7. *Blossoming*: **Seeing beyond disappointment and derision to new opportunity and resolve.**
   How can we remember blossoms of hope when winters of setback and loss seduce us to despair?

8. *Remembering Tanya*: **Grasping the truth of John Donne's paradox that 'Death, thou shalt die.'**
   How brightly does the hope of eternal life in the Kingdom of the Firstborn burn for me?

9. *A Scientist Stays the Course*: **Escaping the trap of trying to be the masters of our own destiny.**
   Of what truth should we be proud and hold dear - will it stand the test of time?

10. *Small Steps and a Giant Leaps* – **In Jesus we can be more than conquerors.**
    Do the deep peace and joy of Jesus sustain and propel me on His missions 'impossible'?

Finding answers means asking more questions and being open, honest and very observant!

- **Each reflection area has a starting point of "backpack resources" to collect and reflect upon. These help one to traverse critical waypoints of the pilgrim's progress.**
- **Pack your personal pilgrim's backpack carefully with the resources that will assist you best navigate the route you must travel through "many dangers, toils and snares." ("Amazing Grace.")**
- **Arrange resources methodically in your mental backpack so that you can quickly access what is important for a particular challenge that you may face suddenly. Are you ready to be authoritative, fluent and persuasive? Test yourself out with others!**
- **There is room in this reflection guide to add your own notes and resource references as well as some personally significant photographs that link your insights to your pilgrim progress.**

1. What is exhilarating and fascinating about a storm? Why?

2. There is no word quite like "supercilious" which means being "superior" but it has the sense of being disdainfully proud and contemptuous of others. Storms are like this. They can shipwreck us in an instant with this sort of aloof capricious danger that has no mercy, knocking puny pride completely out of us. How do I respond to this prospect? What can I learn from potent virus type experiences or sudden accidents that afflict me? How do I get beyond the complaint of 'why me?'

3. How has my pride/humility continuum changed as a result of the storms in my life?

4. What help can I rely on to shelter me from storms?

5. How do storms clarify my priorities for the future? What is important about how we clean up after a storm? E.g. After experiencing Cyclone Althea in Townsville, Australia, December 1971, which tore the roof off our home, our family was so shocked by the massive chaos, that when the house was secured with tarpaulins we wisely escaped some of the tropical deluge that followed and visited relatives and friends in the south, who all noticed our heightened amazement and lingering terror at the destructive power we had witnessed. Many are quite unprepared for the delayed shock of such challenges. This affects our judgement and perspective. Consider the different responses of children and adults. How can an individual or family prepare for disasters? Reflect in relation to physical and also psychological / spiritual crisis/temptation storms.

Pilgrim Back pack Resource 1: Compare and contrast storms in the Bible.

- Jonah 1.
- Matthew 14:22-33 – this is the incident pictured in the mosaic image.
- Luke 8:23-25.
- Acts 27:13-44.

1. When has asserting my independent will resulted in outcomes that I try to block out and veil from others?

2. The melancholic girl of this second poem is the only place in the progress sequence that refers overtly and specifically to the force of evil that the Firstborn warns us about repeatedly. After this the influence goes underground and strikes from behind the scenes throughout the progress. How conscious am I of evil powers at work and how should they be discovered and fought?

3. Consider the distance there is between "anguish" … "grief" and the "merry light of joy." What is my vision and what are my specific goals in relation to how to face the suffering which often veils the work of the Firstborn in healing us?

4. What veils do I need specifically to have lifted? Consider: personal habits, family, work, social groups I frequent, other cultures, world mission/aid.

5. How does focus on the Firstborn lead to lifting what is veiling the truth we need and also dealing with the veils with which we disguise our flaws? Explore how different personality types need varying styles and priorities of encouragement, meditation, reflection and intervention to get to the truth about what really matters for someone? How do we arrest our inclination to hide behind cultivated ignorance?

Pilgrim Backpack Resource 2: Although we hide behind veils, truth is also often veiled for us to seek out – follow the theme of disguises:

- The veil is hung in the temple - Exodus 26:31-33.
- Moses put a veil over his face – Exodus 34:35.
- Prophecy that there will be a way for truth veils to be lifted for all - Isaiah 25:7.
- The tearing of the temple veil - Mark 15:38.
- Following the Firstborn lifts the veil of a hardened heart: 2 Corinthians 3:12–16. Hebrews 10:19-22.
- The stubborn deafness and blindness of many who call themselves God's people but who are not: Acts 28: 23–28. Prophesied long ago in Isaiah 6:9-10. This is a real trap for prospective Christian pilgrims – has our heart become calloused?

1. Is *Luke by the Lake* promoting a rigid early morning devotional ritual for the pilgrim or is it more about questioning the habits we indulge in whereby we rearrange and curtail at a whim to suit ourselves whatever relationship time we have promised the Firstborn, be it morning, noon or evening? The answer to this question gives insight to the depth of our relationship with the Firstborn. So, put another way, do we tend to fit God into our schedule or focus our schedule on the one who will make it succeed so that we do please and glorify Him?

2. Do I ever get into an argument with the one who said "Come let us reason together … though your sins be as scarlet, they shall be whiter than snow…" Isaiah 1:18? Is there a dialogue constantly happening between Jesus and me such that I can sense conscience, experience and memory of teaching from the past bringing back a true perspective and balance? Alternatively, is the line of the "royal telephone" very faint or perhaps even dead? How can the connection be improved?

3. If Jesus really is King of all Kings, do I respect and honour Him as such or do I descend to the over familiar so that that when things get really hard His name is little more than a swear word? What is the remedy?

4. There is an old saying: "if you feel far from God, guess who moved?" How does Jesus love us back?

5. What is the right balance between routine and flexibility in our life patterns when learning to follow the missions of the Firstborn? Is there a guiding principle or simple test to apply here?

Pilgrim Backpack Resource 3 – allowing Jesus to define Himself as King in our lives.
- Colossians 1:15-21 – the Power, Purpose and Friendship of King Jesus. Repays close study.
- The Shocking Alternative by C S Lewis. 2017 doodle doc of his famous BBC talk during the Second World War when he advanced the only three logical conclusions concerning Jesus: Liar, Lunatic or Lord? We must choose : https://youtu.be/bxzuh5Xx5G4
- Who is Jesus? Talk by Billy Graham. 1971. https://youtu.be/U89zkUZPd5w
- Viewed from a secular perspective, Jesus has turned the world upside down – view the You Tube and/or download the script of Jesus the seven way King, talk excerpt by Dr S Lockridge: https://youtu.be/VwQqQkdn_5Q

Reflection Four – Learning to Read and Respond to Creation.

1. Can you remember a special moment whilst pushing onwards through the humdrum of your progress that you were suddenly stopped in your tracks by a radiant rainbow, some breathtakingly glorious scenery, or an intricate microcosm of fern and insect that suddenly transcended what was ordinary for you? Imagine this again for a few moments. Try to smell, hear, touch and see it. Then:

   • Did time seem to stop for you? Why?

   • Were you overcome by a canvas of colour and shape that was inconceivably majestic and awesome? Examples?

   • Did you wonder about there being a Creator of this and what such a being was like? What was the result of this wonder for you?

   • Did you have to search for words to describe to others later what was at first indescribable? What words would you use now for this?

   • Does this sort of experience <u>not</u> happen for you and do you find little response to such things? Why?

2. The poem "Palmetum Musing" focuses on a tightly knit group of distracted teenagers dominated by powerful peer group patterns. The busload of rowdy students on the outward journey to attempt creative writing at a beautiful Palmetum oasis surrounded by drought conditions, is thoroughly distracted and insensitive to whatever may be learned from such an experience. Their empty, insular banter reflects the arid conditions of many life patterns and outlooks that can often mask what is glorious.

   What are your distractions? Consider:

   • Group pressures to conform to traditions so as to belong to others.

   • My habits of behaviour: task orientation or lack thereof.

   • My motivations of greed, lust, status, jealousy, revenge and power over others that swamp sensitivity.

   • My focus on thrills from daring do or just searching out what is weird and quirky. E.g. On the internet.

3. What is needed to break the hold that negative distractions have over me so that I can begin to appreciate the wonders of the universe? Why should I even bother to explore further? Start with some calculation and reflection on the probability of natural creation occurring by chance. How were the teenagers in the poem helped? Can this happen to me? How? What are the conditions for this?

4. Universally in the global village of today, both natural beauty and disaster are attributed to "Mother Nature." Often this is conveyed in a patronising, disparaging way – what is she up to next? Why is such a myth so prevalent? On what basis does our modern age refer to this mother god?

5. Now examine Pilgrim Backpack Resource 4 and your own research to explore the creation claims of the omnipotent designer God revealed in His word. He says His name is simply but potently "I am." (Exodus 3:14.) The Psalmist exudes: "you created every part of me" and "before I even speak you already know what I will say." Psalm 139: 4.

   How does the dawn of the certainty of God's amazing creation change our outlook on life? As we grow up, how can such certainty be nurtured?

   Consider the implications of an observation by Amanda Penland:

   "Walk around outside with a child and you will find out how beautiful God's creations are."

   What changes do you need to make to increase perception of the Creator in His creation?

Pilgrim Backpack Resource 4 – knowing the great designer God from the wonder of His creation.

- Psalms: 8:3–6; 19:1-6 33:6 95:4-5; 104:24, 25; 121:1-2; 139:1–18.
- Isaiah 40:28. Amos 9:6
- Romans 1:20. Hebrews 11:3
- Romans 8:19-21 – What is the future for the creation that has been scarred by humans?
- Many poets repay close reading from this perspective – e.g. start with Gerald Manly Hopkins: "God's Grandeur" and "Pied Beauty." Also William Wordsworth's revelations in poems such as "Composed Upon Westminster Bridge."

  Check and affirm for yourself regularly that: "The world is charged with the grandeur of God." As you journey forward look closely at the wonders of nature for this grandeur "will flame out, like shining from shook foil." (From "God's Grandeur") Do you see this shining out?

1. In "Heavy Homecoming", there is the deep sadness that many have missed finding the secret of the plan of salvation from evil that is gifted to us under the new covenant, whereby they could be reborn with Jesus into His Kingdom of light and righteousness. Why was this plan such a carefully guarded secret?

   The prophets knew there was a plan but the 'when' and 'how' of it was so secret that even the angels longed to know it (1 Peter 1:12) and Jesus Himself in the garden questioned the way forward and prayed asking for another way. (Matthew 26:39). For the plan to work, certain conditions had to be in place but the great designer God knew for certain they would indeed be there and that the forces of evil could be defeated as a result of their own horrific cruelty and injustice. So a hypothetical long chance became a divine certainty that was known to the Father before time began.

   What needed to happen and be in place for the Firstborn's rescue mission to be successful and so justify its initial secrecy and bring about the way back to God that was lost in Eden?

2. As we believe in Jesus as Lord, and trust and obey Him into the future, we become His sister or brother – we are welcomed so intimately into a loving, royal, divine family of the King of Kings. Our earthly families are imperfect. How then can we get a true picture of what it is like to join God's family? A good starting point for this is Paul's well-known "Living in the Light" section of his letter to the Ephesians – chapter 5: 1–20, especially the last three verses of this.

3. The execution cross is a seemingly impossible symbol for Jesus the King of Kings, and it remains a great affront to many religious people to this day. Yet followers of the Firstborn must also deny themselves and take up their particular cross if they are to follow Jesus. (Matthew 16: 24-26). How should this symbol find significance and use in our lifetime? How is the heavy homecoming of our saviour Jesus different to ours? How is ours similar to His?

4. In reflecting on the cruel death of the Firstborn coming home about 33 years after the miraculous gift of Him being conceived in Mary by the Holy Spirit, what is revealed of the character of this young human being who learned that he was both man and God at the same time? What do we need to emulate here?

5. If such a wonderful salvation cannot be earned by good works but is a free gift received by belief, evidenced in submission of our will to that of the Firstborn, why do so many reject it? What specific things can we know are the eternal consequences of this? (See Romans 6:22-23 and Hebrews 2:1-4)

Pilgrim Backpack Resource 5 – Heirs with the Firstborn.

- Romans 5:1-11. Romans 8:12 – 17. Ephesians 2:8 -10 & 19-22.

- John 17 – The success of the rescue mission – assessment by the Firstborn Himself. Plan debrief before the bloody climax to 'mission impossible'! Consider the amazing calm and supreme confidence of the Firstborn on the eve of execution, utterly certain that although His followers will "have trouble in the world" that they progress through as pilgrims, they can "take heart" for He had "overcome the world." John 16:33.

- Stuart Townend's poignant song: "How Deep the Father's Love for us"

- Joni Eareckson Tada testimony – she was a quadriplegic at 17 and after 50 years 'bearing her cross' in a wheelchair she has now become a renowned artist, speaker, author and also a great mover to help the disabled. Check out the books about her and her talks. Her impressive rich walk with the Firstborn is inspiring and challenging as she now says that she would not have wanted her life any other way.

1. How realistic do you find is the cross-cultural unity of all who truly love the Firstborn? Examples?

2. How is this unity nurtured and protected? To start with, see Ephesians 4:1-6.

3. As we mature, how does our appreciation and initiative to protect unity grow and manifest itself?

4. What are some important precursors either for an initial starting point to trust the Firstborn or for revival?

5. What needs to happen in the aftermath of such a mighty move of God's Spirit? Are we ready?

Pilgrim Backpack Resource 6 – **All one in Christ**

- Ephesians 2: 11-22 – Jew v Gentile racism is finished – all 'Berlin walls' are down with Jesus.

- Mat 24: 14 and Mark 13:10 – The Firstborn will not return until the gospel is communicated to the whole world. We are warned not to look for dates but nevertheless look forward alert to be ready for the return of the Firstborn, whenever this might be.

- Explore the progress of world Christian mission and revival to test the "swell of gospel love chorus." E.g.
  View the vast resources of Operation World: www.operationworld.org . Started in 1964 for prayer groups in Africa, it became a serious globalised investigation by 1974 and now it is passed its 7th edition published in 2010. This encyclopaedic work examines the state of outreach of the gospel in every country in the world. There are separate volumes for major countries like China with its "hidden" minority groups. The gospel is known in most corners of the globe but quite a few small ethnic groups are still almost totally unreached with news of the hope of the Firstborn for them.
  Use this for prayers that all may be reached as a matter of high priority.
  Do you see some relevance of this to your being called to some aspect of global outreach for Jesus?

Reflection Seven – the hope that takes us beyond disappointment and despair.

1. When faced with sad winters how important is it to prioritize retreat? What principles guide this?
2. What can we do in the times of blossom, hope and plenty to prepare for sad winters of setback?
3. What are the advantages and dangers of taking a long term view such as in **Ecclesiastes 3: 1-15**?
4. What are healthy strategies to assist those dealing with spiritual depression?
5. How does the imagery of blossoms help us to aspire to flourish likewise spiritually?

Pilgrim Backpack Resource 7 – Renewal.

- The famous Prayer of Habakkuk – chapter 3 of his prophecy especially v18 – 19. We can rejoice even when there is no fruit or apparent well-being because God is our saviour who gives strength to all the followers of the Firstborn.
- John 16:33. 2 Corinthians 4:7–12. We may be troubled but we will never be crushed by this world's woes because the Firstborn has overcome them.

- Read the amazing letter written by 16-year-old Lady Jane Grey commending the importance of the Bible and Firstborn faithfulness to her less resolute 14 year old sister Katherine, the night before Jane was executed on the 12 February 1554, for refusing to renounce her dependency on this same Word of God. She was only Queen for nine days in the summer of 1553 and although deserted by her family, she stood quite firm in following the Firstborn through dark days of an incredibly wintry experience to find the glorious blossom of a certain place by faith in His eternal Kingdom:

- "Now as touching my death, rejoice as I do, my dearest sister, that I shall be delivered of this corruption, and put on incorruption: for I am assured that I shall, for losing of a mortal life, win one that is immortal, joyful, and everlasting: the which I pray God grant you in his most blessed hour, and send you his all-saving grace to love in his fear, and to die in the true Christian faith."

- Subject of many references but notably read expressively with commentary by writer Philippa Gregory - https://youtu.be/-a51WWN87i0

- Be soothed by some of the many Christian songs about perfect peace as you walk alongside the Firstborn. e.g. Tommy Walker's *The Peace of Christ:* https://youtu.be/WN9bEkGe6ss and Laura Story's *Perfect Peace:* https://youtu.be/7UpfatdyFtY

1. What sort of natural human thoughts and emotions are experienced in the face of death?
2. How does the gospel speak to our grieving process and help us make sense of what has happened?
3. How should we express this to others, especially children?
4. How should we respond to a life cut very short or death when a major work is still unfinished?
5. What balance is needed between the funereal trappings of death and the hope of eternal life?

Pilgrim Backpack Resource 8 – **Death has lost its sting.**

- John 10:22-30. John 14:1-3. John 20:11-17 – Safe forever in the perfect care of the Firstborn.
- Revelation 21:1-8. The new heaven and the new earth together always with the Firstborn.
- 1 Corinthians 15:51-58. Death is destroyed.
- "Death be Not Proud" – famous poem by John Donne. Victory over death.
- *A Severe Mercy* – fascinating autobiography of American Sheldon Vanauken, who received 18 letters from CS Lewis in Oxford to help him through the tragic lingering death of his wife. Both were helped.
- *Death has lost its Sting*- hymn by Isaac Watts based on Psalm 3 with modern adaptions: the focus point is the affirmation: 'Terror no more will shake my soul, My refuge is my God."

1. What are some different motivations to initiate discovery in the created order? What matters most?

2. Why is the process of discovery best "forged with awe"?

3. In what ways today do we suffer from the arrogant pride behind much scientific endeavour?

4. How can science lead us both towards and away from the Firstborn?

5. What use of science best delights and pleases both the Firstborn and His Father?

Pilgrim Backpack Resource 9 – **Eternity of truth** – a heavy load to carry here. Research with care!

- Genesis 1:26-31 – What is the meaning and significance of us being made in the image of God? Investigate this with reference to the Scientific Method, which uses six steps to find truth.

- Examine the case for the person, work and supremacy of the Firstborn by one of the eminent evangelical scientist Christians of the last hundred years. A good example would be:

  A Scientist in God's World – 1978 paper by eminent British physicist Prof Donald Mackay (quoted in *The Open Mind*, IVP 1988) in which he argues cogently that "a scientist in God's world who knows and loves the Author of it can rejoice equally in the growth of the explanatory structure of science and in any surprises that might shake it." (Page 31 of *The Open Mind*). This is a dense, challenging read but Prof Mackay shows how really even the most solid looking things are in flux and this is consistent with them being held together by a self-sufficient Creator who can change "natural precedents" as appropriate for significant events such as the resurrection. He sees these events as quite consistent with the real essence of science and argues that "what is completely unjustified, is the suggestion that scientific explanation rationally warrants *disbelief* in the Creator." (Page 28 of *The Open Mind*).

- Mars Surface Rovers are exploring Martian terrain not just for what is actually there but for traces of life which has always been a perennial theme of space exploration. Why this distraction by scientists away from legitimate, objective exploration and discovery to an unscientific preoccupation with alien life forms, for which there is no substantial evidence? Research, explore and explain what insights are

revealed by this expensive application of science. Compare with the biblical imperative that we should prioritise our exploration to find, not Martians but contentment and fulfilment in relationship with the creator of the universe: Psalm 34:10b. Philippians 4:11-13. 1 Timothy 6:6-12. 2 Corinthians 12:9-10. We quickly find that to do this requires a complete mental transformation – see Romans 12:2.

- If you get confused about the consistency of scientific endeavour and friendship with the Firstborn, a good clarifying corrective is to read from the concise, incisive thoughts (Pensees) of the great French scientist Blaise Pascal, whose short but brilliant life was marked by a close following of the Firstborn. His notebook of Pensees is most enlightening. For example, thought number 417 of the second part of his Apology is a remarkable conclusion for many today as it comes from an experimental scientist:

   "We only know ourselves through Jesus Christ; we only know life and death through Jesus Christ. Apart from Jesus Christ we cannot know the meaning of our life and death, of God or ourselves. Thus without Scripture, whose only object is Christ, we know nothing, and can see nothing but obscurity and confusion in the nature of God and in nature itself."

1. How do we know what our mission might be?
2. How do we see the vision beyond our small steps to the giant leaps forward with the Spirit?
3. What sacrifices might we be called to make and are they worth it?
4. In my mission am I 'zooming home' or being dragged with reluctant feet? What change is needed?
5. What are the blessings both to myself and to others in undertaking missions for the Firstborn?

Pilgrim Backpack Resource 10 – **Mission accomplished.**

- Matthew 25:19-21 –well done faithful servant – a preparation for what is to come.

- John 15:11-17 – now firm friends with the Firstborn, experiencing joy and learning more and more of the Kingdom as we abide in love.

- Revelation 22:1-5 – We will see the face of the Firstborn and there will be no more curse of evil.

- Choose one of the hundreds of Christian missionary stories where this hope of fellowship with the Firstborn has been shared successfully across a culture such that evil has been defeated and the 'hope of glory' kindled.

   e.g. For my parents, this was a personal involvement from 1951 with the East Malaysian Borneo Evangelical Mission, whose story to reach animistic head hunters starts in 1928 and has been told by Hudson Southwell, one of its three Australian co-founders, in his autobiography *Unchartered Waters*, Astana 1973. The BEM moved to became a totally self-supporting indigenous church after it was renamed in 1959 as Sidang Injil Borneo. This was four years after my parents left their mission work there to settle in Australia. The mission accomplished its goals and now the S.I.B shares the gospel throughout East Malaysia with no more need of expatriate help.

   There are many other inspiring and exciting stories of missions 'impossible but for the work of the Spirit'.

FOR FURTHER READING:

1. ***The Pilgrim's Progress from This World, to That Which Is to Come*** - 1678 Christian allegory written by John Bunyan. It has been regarded as the first 'novel' written in English.

2. The Lausanne Covenant - The *Lausanne Covenant* is 'widely regarded as one of the most significant documents in modern church history.' (See the internet!) Emerging from the First Lausanne Congress in 1974, with renowned biblical scholar and writer John Stott as its chief architect, it serves as a great rallying call to Christians around the world, who rely on the bible as the Word of God. It defines what it means to be a Christian pilgrim today, and challenges Christians to work together to make Jesus Christ known throughout the world.

3. The short answer to these weighty questions about progressing as a pilgrim is John 3:16:
   "For God so loved the world that he gave his one and only Son, that whoever believes in him shall not perish but have eternal life."

ACKNOWLEDGEMENTS

My thanks to:

- My parents, family and mentors who have taught me much about following the Firstborn.
- My dear wife Ellen for her faithful advice and encouragement through hours of work on this book.
- Peter Rainey and John Kennedy, two university lecturers from the English Department of James Cook University where I trained, who have encouraged and helped me check and edit the poetry.
- Rhondda Long, a student contemporary from those University days of the seventies, who shared her responses to the poetry and made helpful suggestions.
- Olympus cameras. They make excellent lenses and I used two Olympus cameras to take the photographs in this book - both a small waterproof, shockproof Olympus TG6 Digital and an E-M10 Mark III SLR Digital with a selection of lenses. Both cameras have performed extremely well, even in very rough field conditions.
- My Triune God for awesome guidance and tender care throughout my odyssey following Him. Psalm 119:54 sums it all up: "Your principles have been the music of my life throughout the years of my pilgrimage."

www.ingramcontent.com/pod-product-compliance
Lightning Source LLC
Chambersburg PA
CBHW041949080426

42735CB00004B/144